Connect the dots from 0 to 5.
Color the picture.

Connect the dots from 0 to 5. Start at the ★. Color the picture.

CD-104332 © Carson-Dellosa

Connect the dots from 0 to 5. Start at the ★.
Color the picture.

Connect the dots from 0 to 5. Start at the ★.
Color the picture.

CD-104332

Connect the dots from 0 to 5. Start at the ★.
Color the picture.

Connect the dots from 0 to 5. Start at the ★.
Color the picture.

CD-104332 © Carson-Dellosa

Connect the dots from 0 to 5. Start at the ★. Color the picture.

0 ★

5

1•

2

3

•4

Connect the dots from 0 to 5. Start at the ★.
Color the picture.

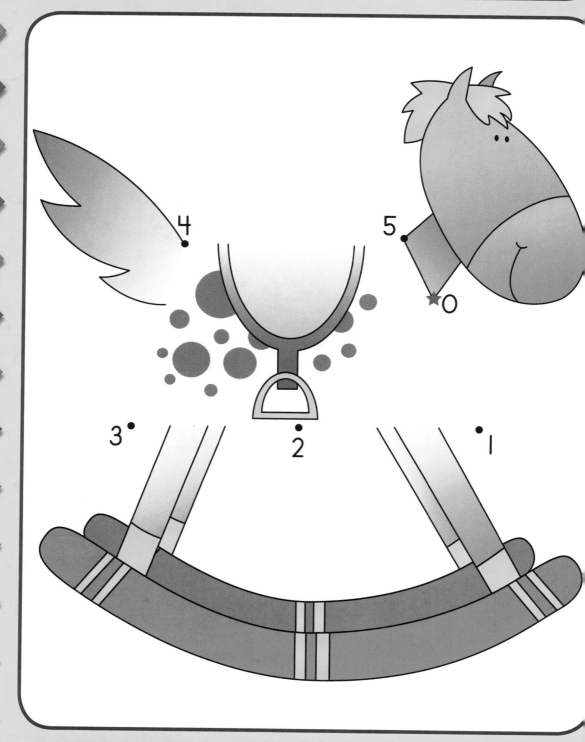

CD-104332

Connect the dots from 0 to 5. Start at the ★. Color the picture.

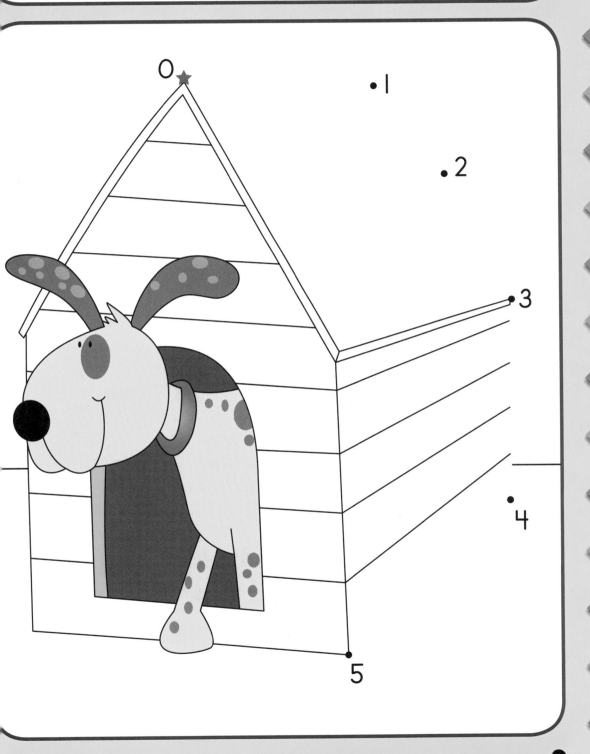

Connect the dots from 0 to 5. Start at the ★.
Color the picture.

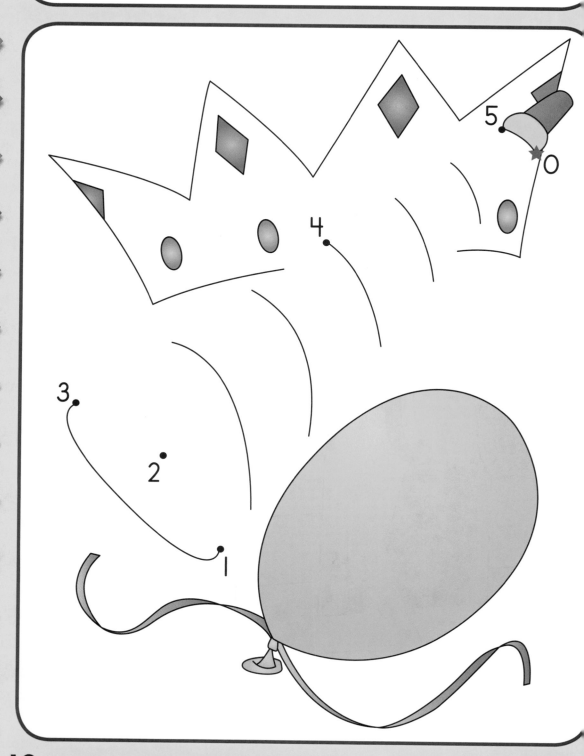

CD-104332

Connect the dots from 0 to 10. Start at the ★. Color the picture.

Connect the dots from 0 to 10. Start at the ★. Color the picture.

CD-104332

Connect the dots from 0 to 10. Start at the ★.
Color the picture.

 CD-104332 **15**

**Connect the dots from 0 to 10. Start at the ★.
Color the picture.**

CD-104332   © Carson-Dellosa

Connect the dots from 0 to 10. Start at the ★.
Color the picture.

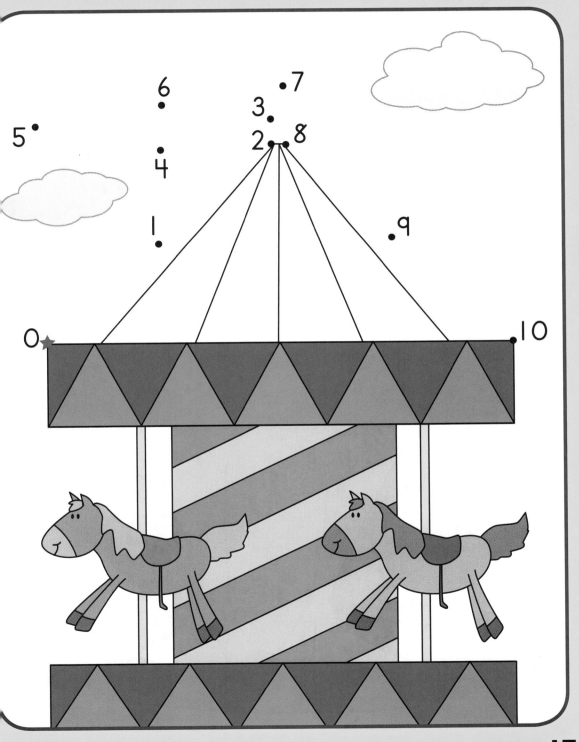

Connect the dots from 0 to 10. Start at the ★. Color the picture.

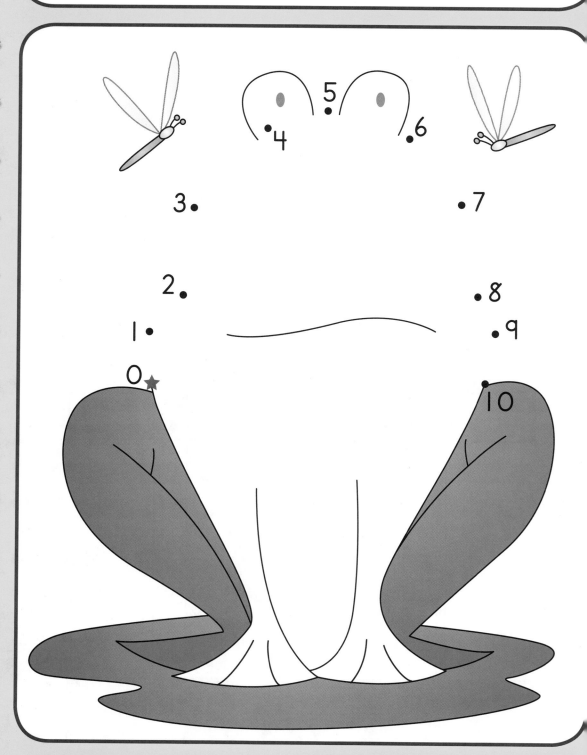

CD-104332

Connect the dots from 0 to 10. Start at the ★. Color the picture.

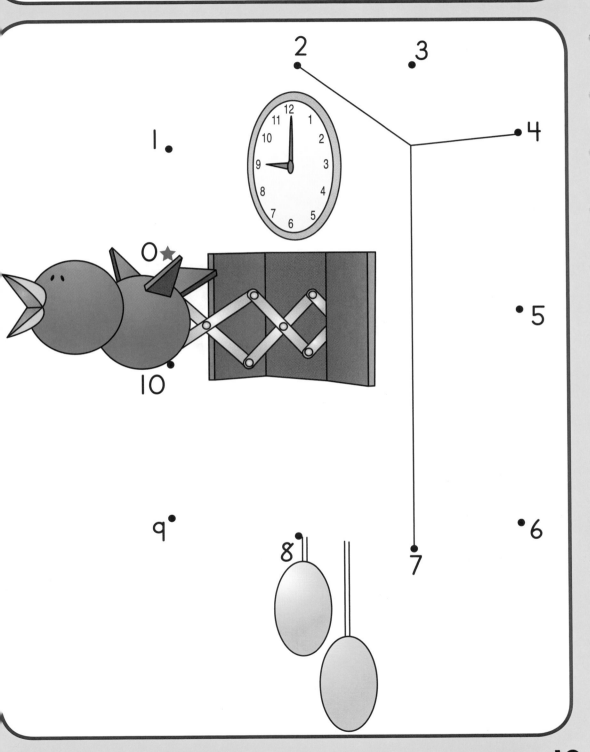

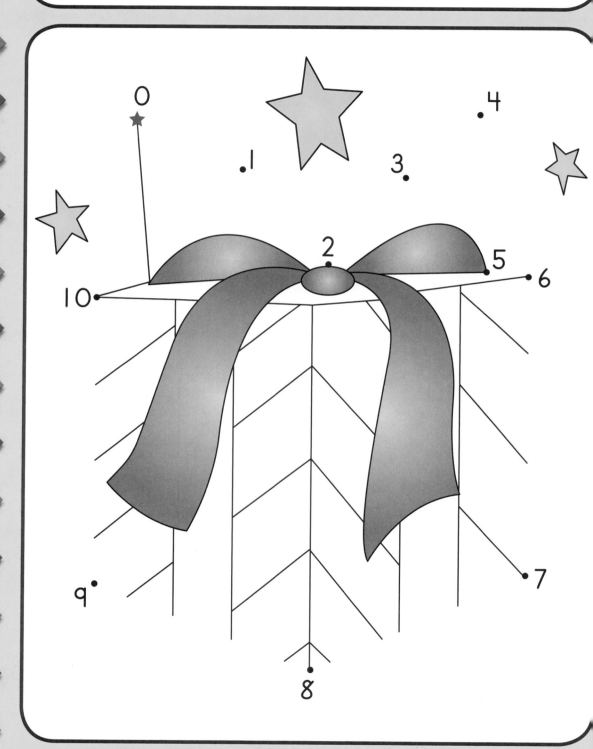

Connect the dots from 0 to 15. Start at the ★.
Color the picture.

CD-104332

Connect the dots from 0 to 15. Start at the ★.
Color the picture.

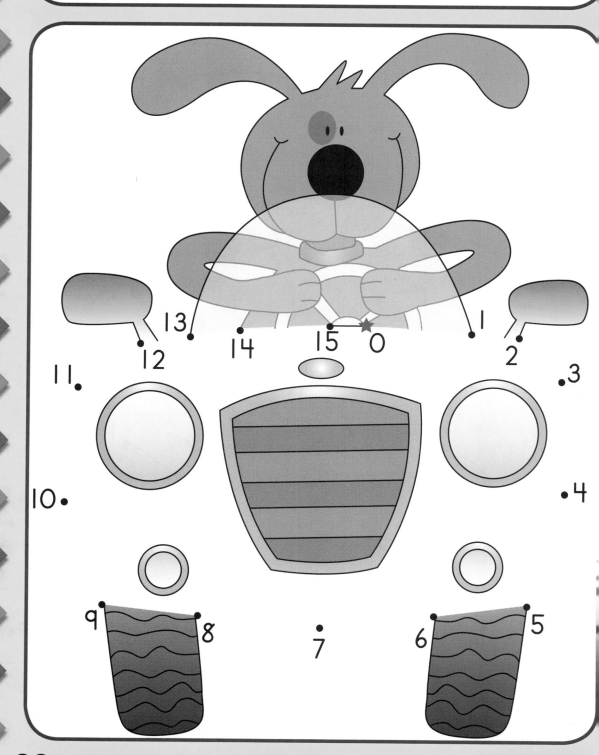

CD-104332 © Carson-Dellosa

Connect the dots from 0 to 15. Start at the ★.
Color the picture.

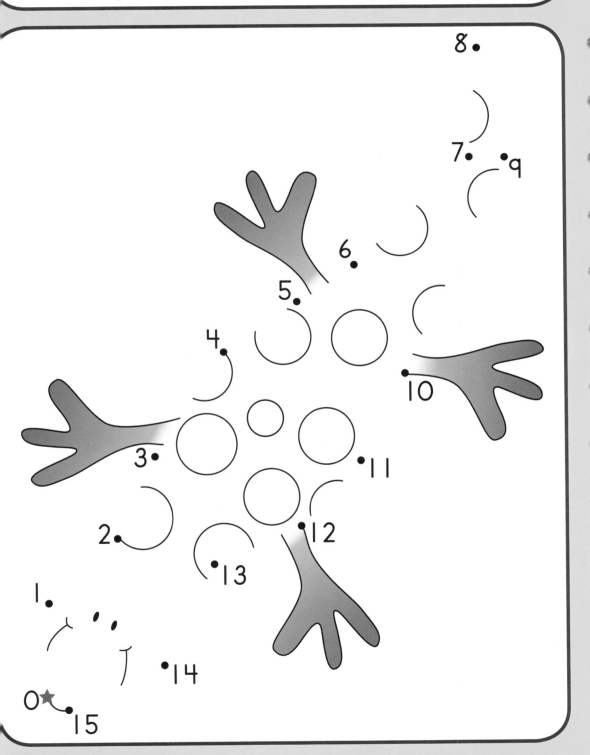

Connect the dots from 0 to 15. Start at the ★.
Color the picture.

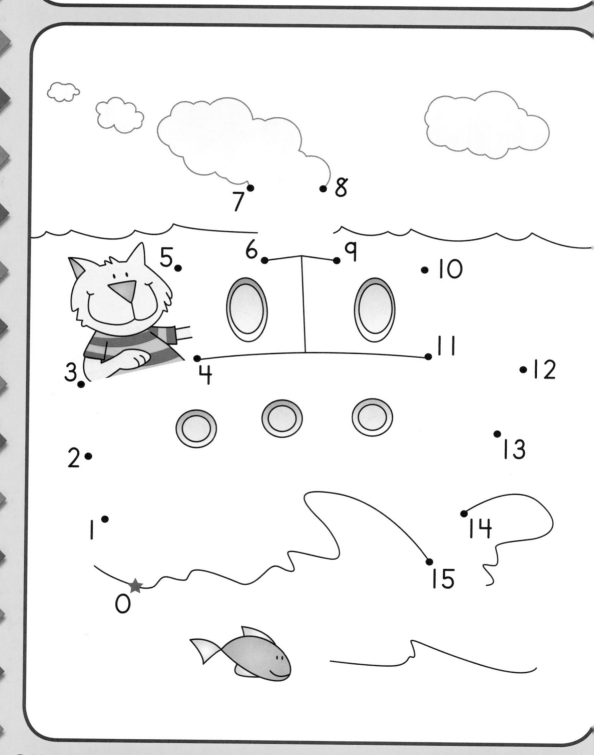

CD-104332 © Carson-Dellosa

Connect the dots from 0 to 15. Start at the ★.
Color the picture.

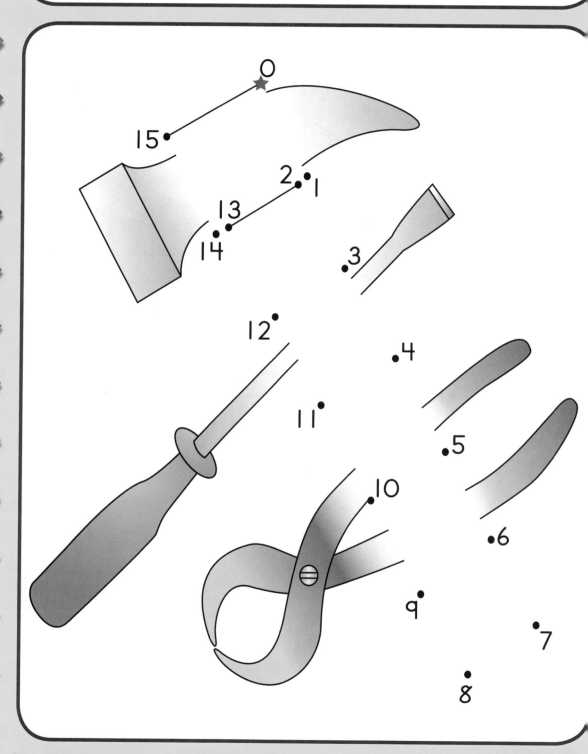

CD-104332

© Carson-Dellosa

Connect the dots from 0 to 15. Start at the ★.
Color the picture.

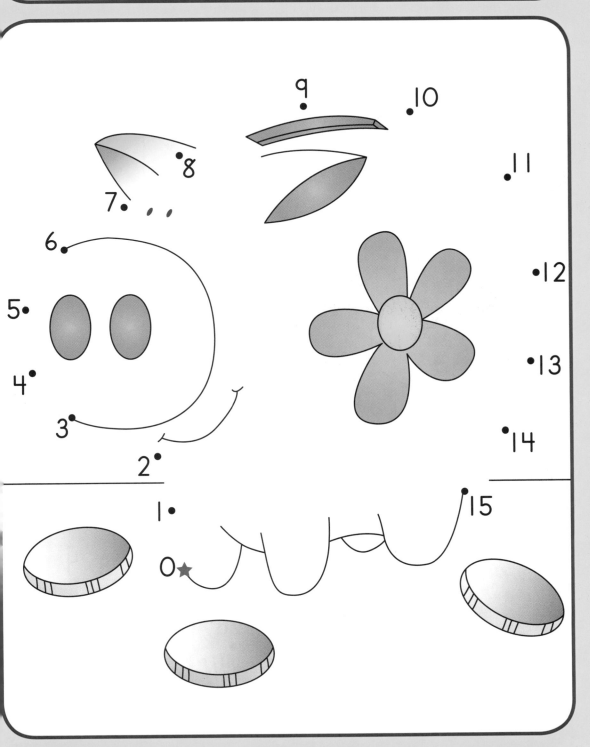

CD-104332

27

Connect the dots from 0 to 15. Start at the ★.
Color the picture.

CD-104332

Connect the dots from 0 to 15. Start at the ★.
Color the picture.

CD-104332 **29**

Connect the dots from 0 to 15. Start at the ★. Color the picture.

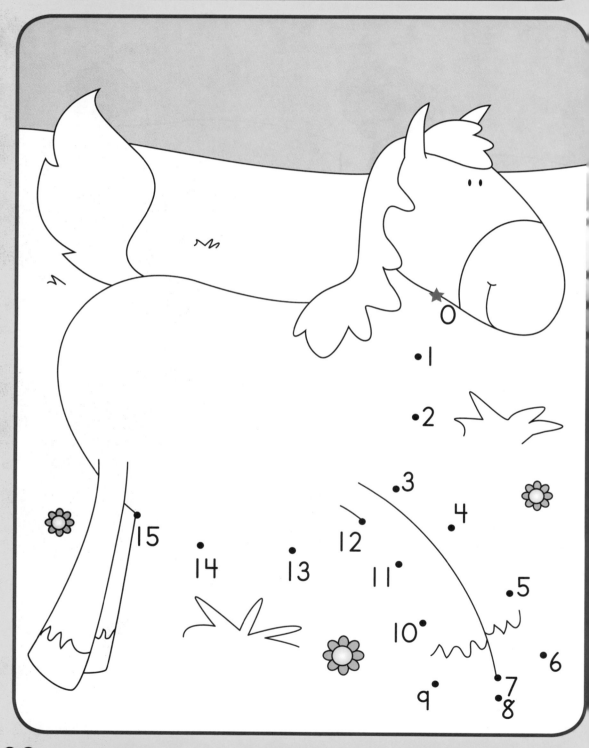

CD-104332

31

Connect the dots from 0 to 20. Start at the ★.
Color the picture.

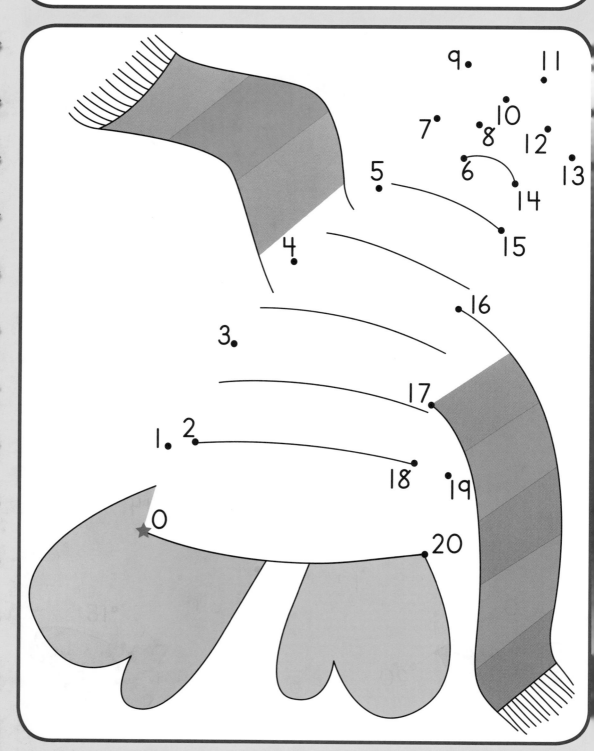

CD-104332 © Carson-Dellosa

Connect the dots from 0 to 20. Start at the ★.
Color the picture.

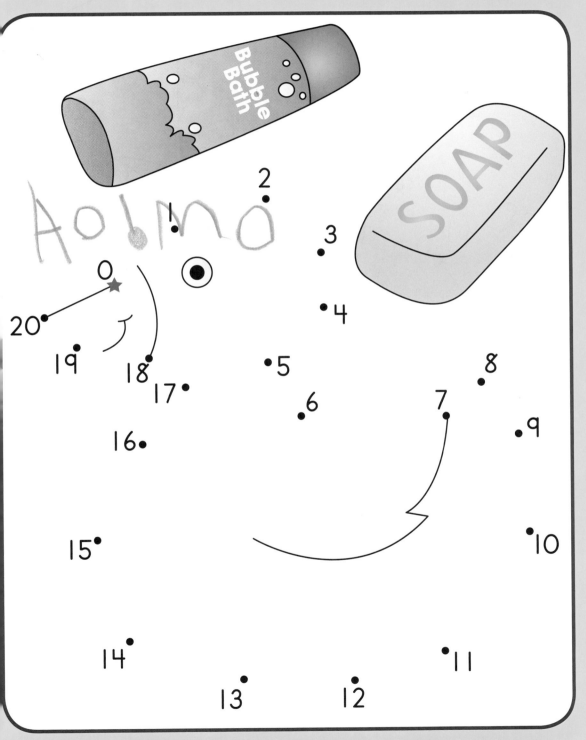

Connect the dots from 0 to 20. Start at the ★. Color the picture.

CD-104332 © Carson-Dellosa

Connect the dots from 0 to 20. Start at the ★. Color the picture.

Connect the dots from 0 to 20. Start at the ★.
Color the picture.

CD-104332
© Carson-Dellosa

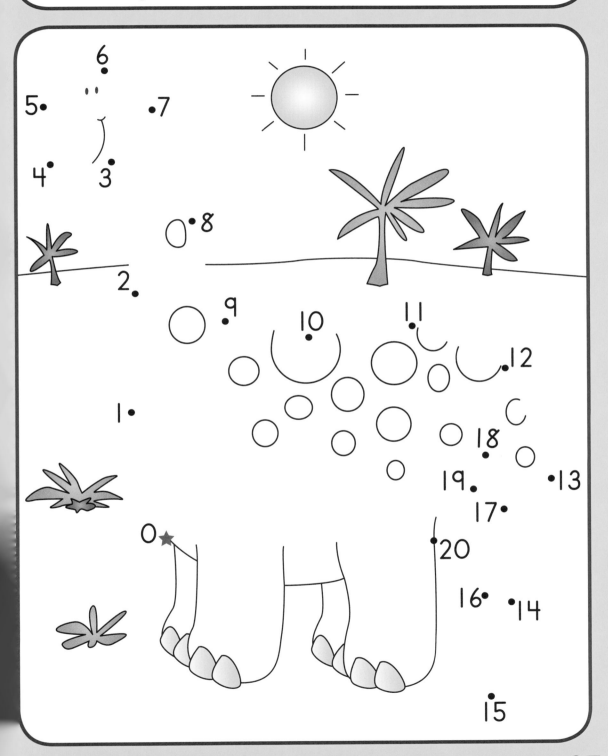

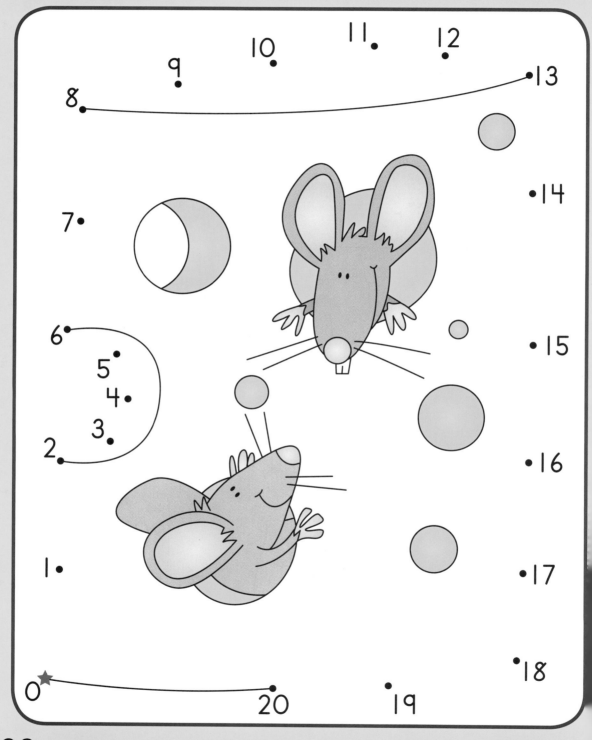

38 CD-104332

© Carson-Dellosa

Connect the dots from 0 to 20. Start at the ★.
Color the picture.

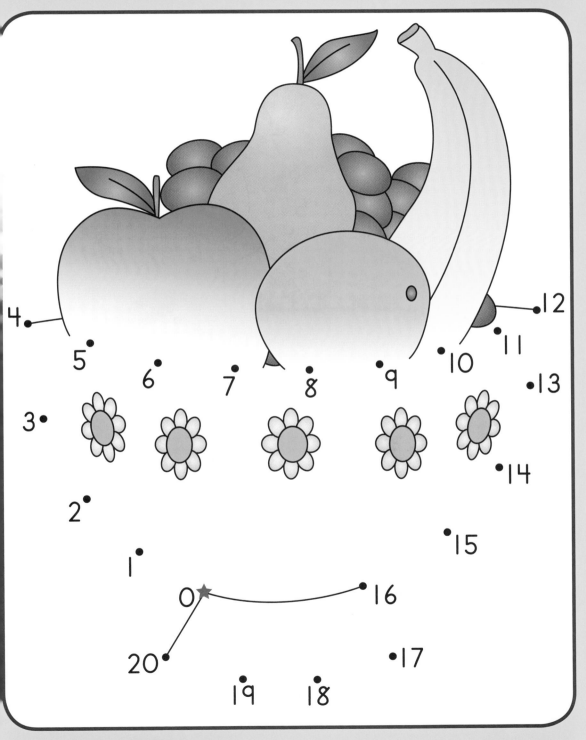

Connect the dots from 0 to 25. Start at the ★.
Color the picture.

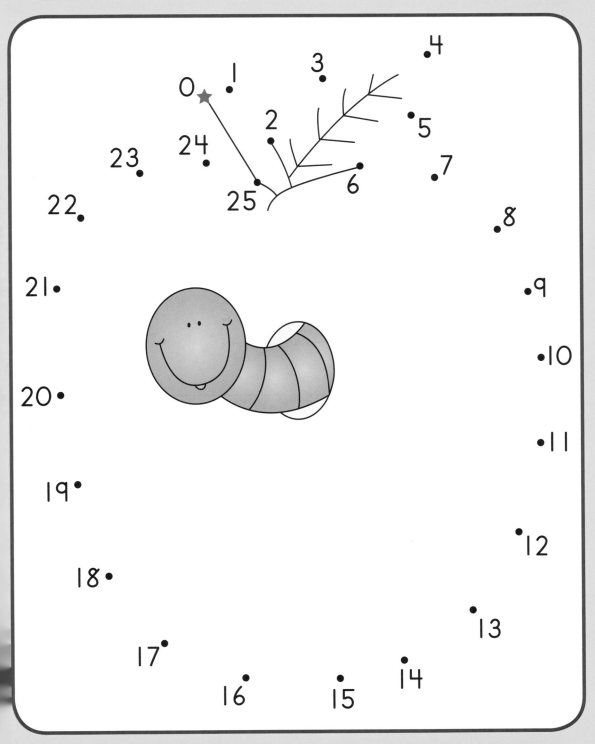

 CD-104332

Connect the dots from 0 to 25. Start at the ★.
Color the picture.

CD-104332 © Carson-Dellosa

Connect the dots from 0 to 25. Start at the ★.
Color the picture.

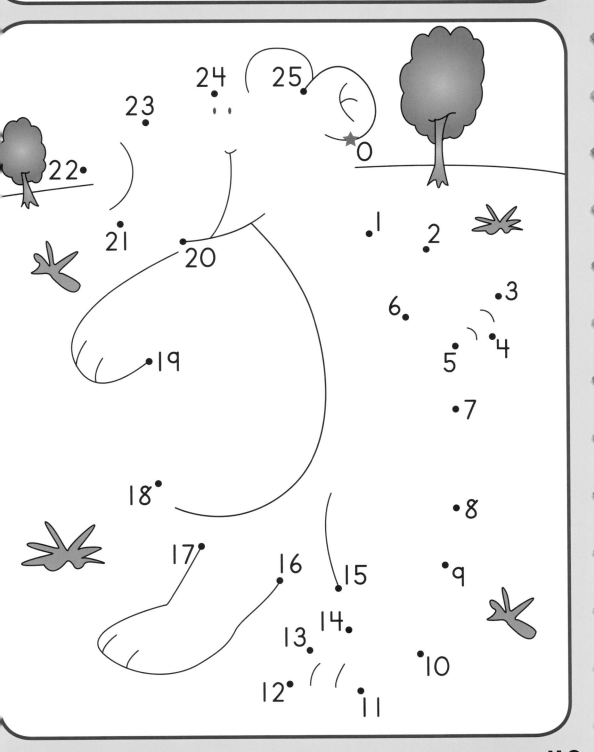

CD-104332

43

**Connect the dots from 0 to 25. Start at the ★.
Color the picture.**

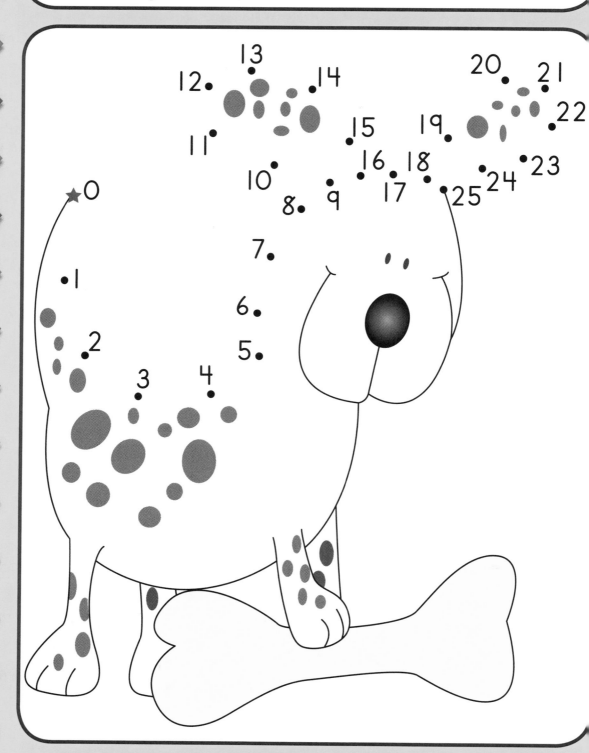

CD-104332 © Carson-Dellosa

Connect the dots from 0 to 25. Start at the ★. Color the picture.

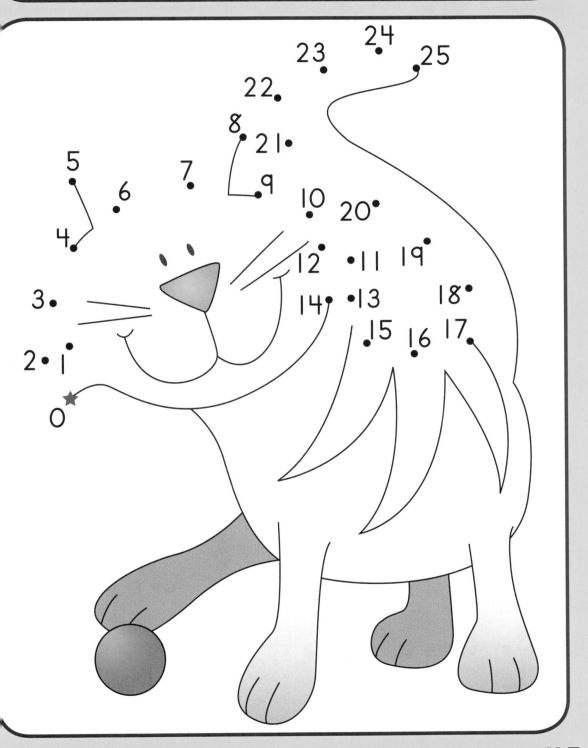

Connect the dots from 0 to 25. Start at the ★. Color the picture.

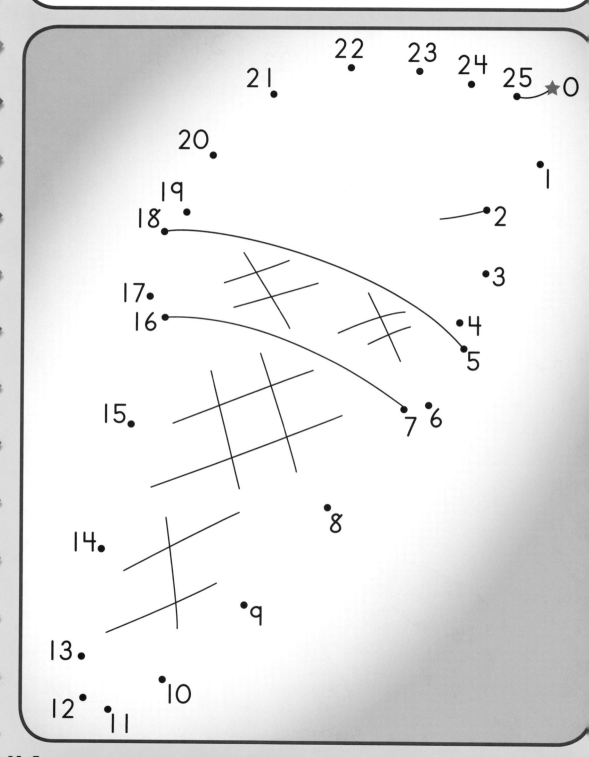

CD-104332

© Carson-Dellosa

Connect the dots from 0 to 25. Start at the ★.
Color the picture.

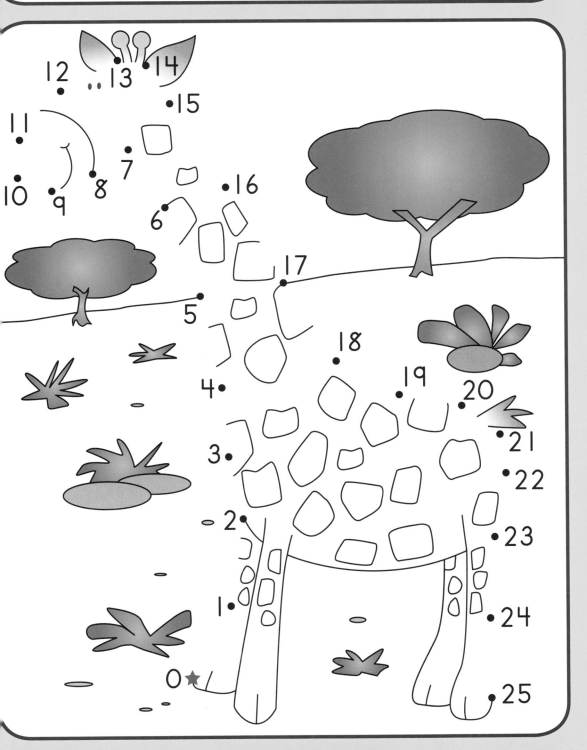

Connect the dots from 0 to 25. Start at the ★.
Color the picture.

CD-104332   © Carson-Dellosa

Connect the dots from 0 to 25. Start at the ★.
Color the picture.

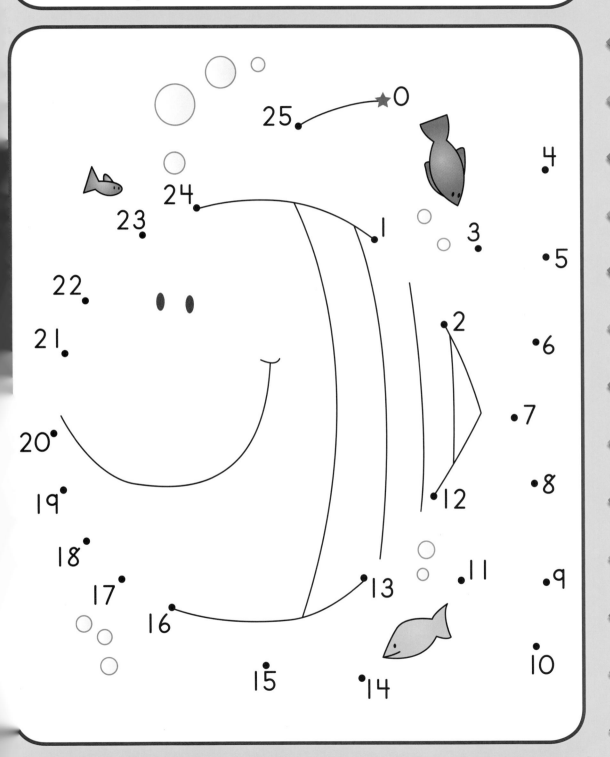

Connect the dots from 0 to 25. Start at the ★.
Color the picture.

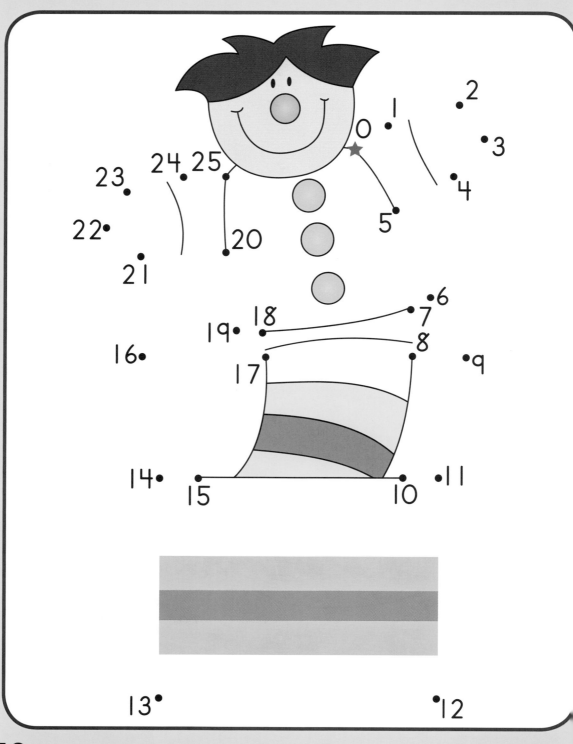

Connect the dots from 0 to 30. Start at the ★. Color the picture.

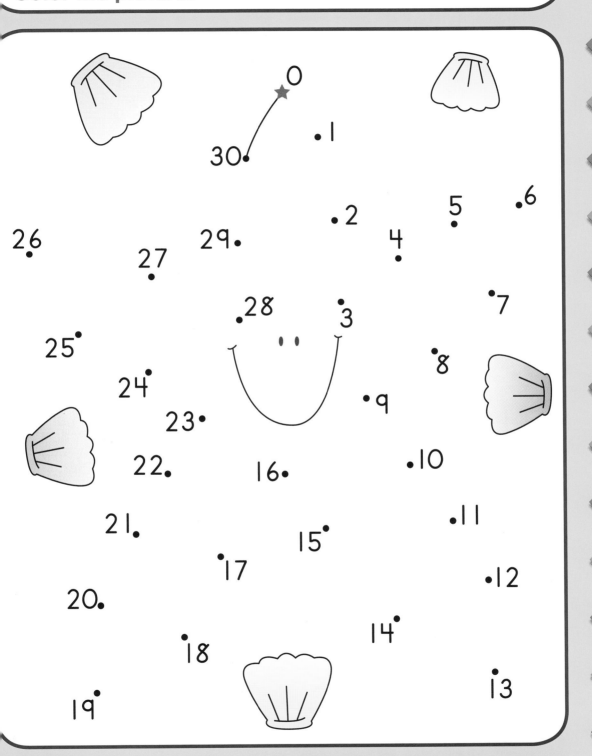

Connect the dots from **0** to **30**. Start at the ★.
Color the picture.

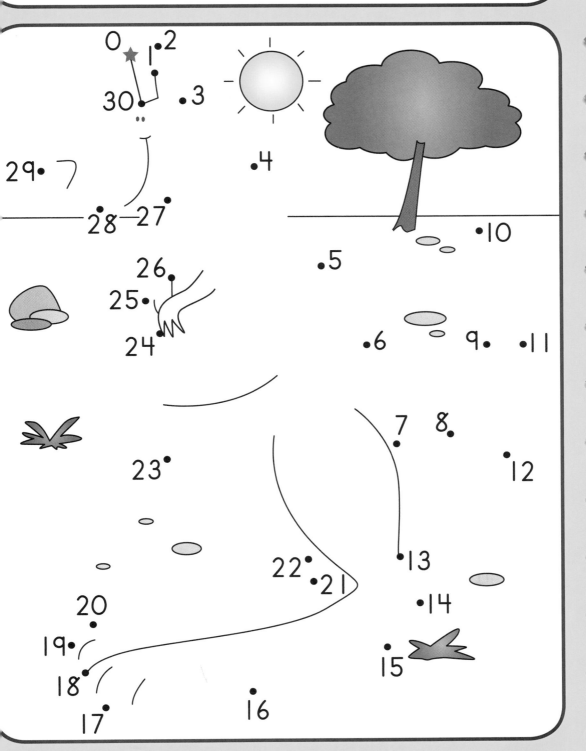

Connect the dots from 0 to 30. Start at the ★. Color the picture.

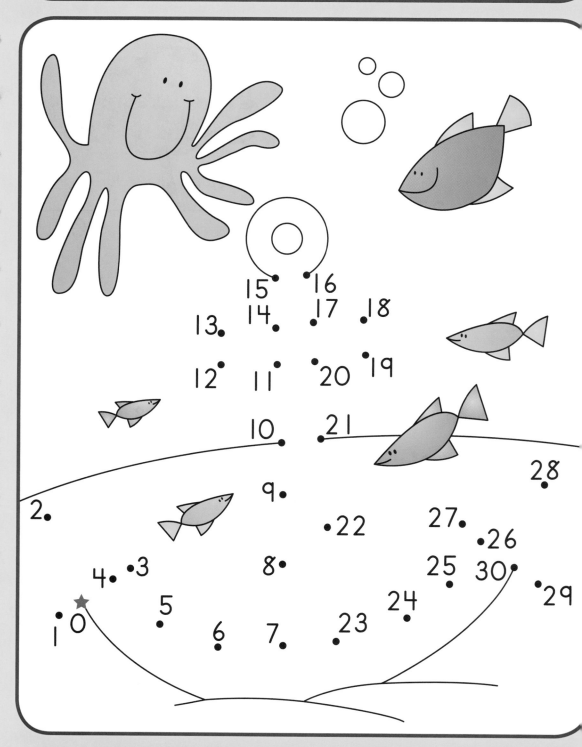

Connect the dots from 0 to 30. Start at the ★.
Color the picture.

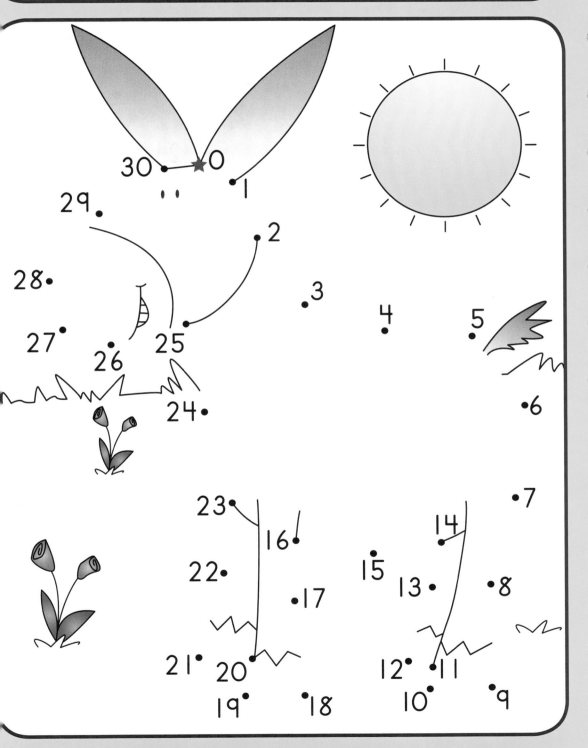

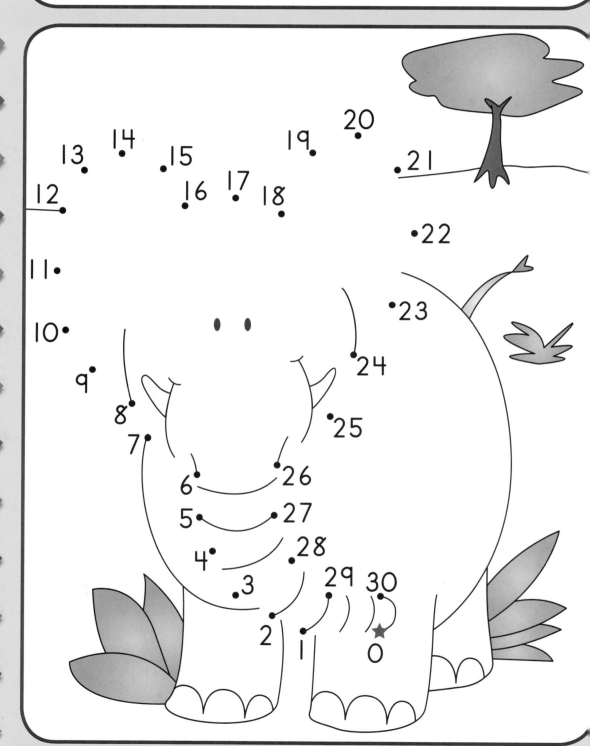

Connect the dots from 0 to 30. Start at the ★.
Color the picture.

CD-104332

Connect the dots from 0 to 30. Start at the ★. Color the picture.

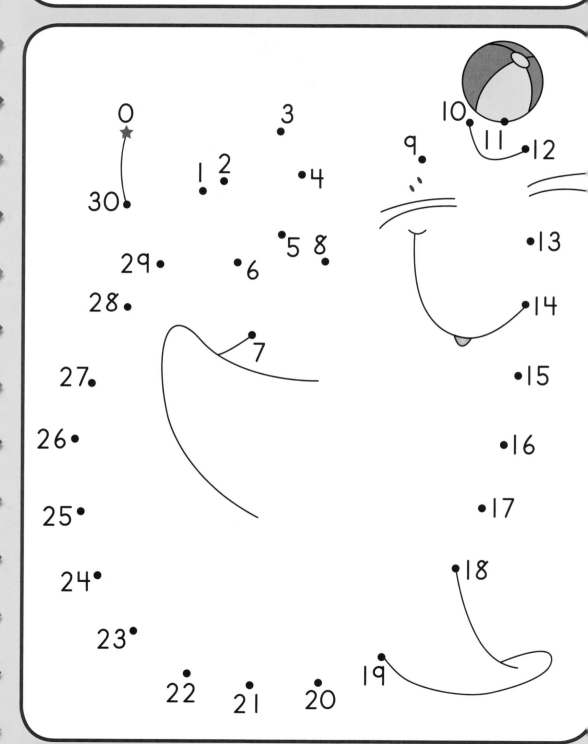

CD-104332 © Carson-Dellosa

Connect the dots from 5 to 15. Start at the ★. Color the picture.

Connect the dots from 5 to 20. Start at the ★. Color the picture.

Connect the dots from 10 to 20. Start at the ★. Color the picture.

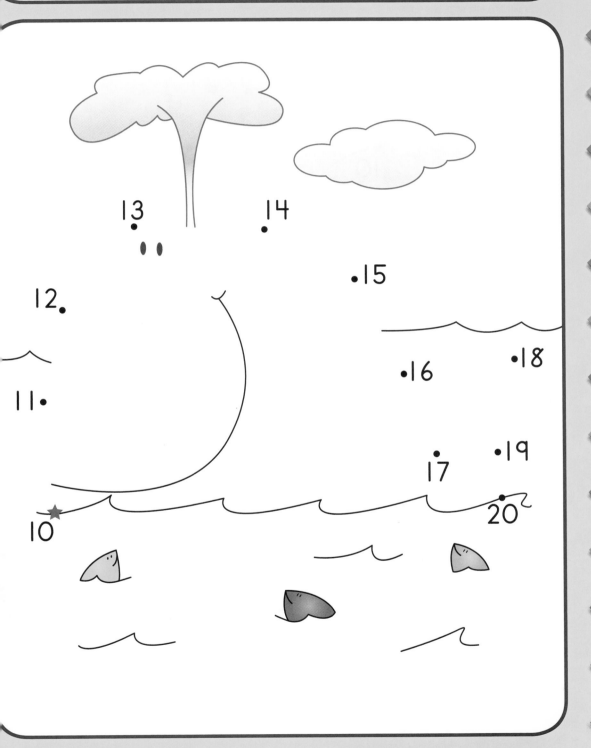

13

14

•15

12.

•18

•16

11•

•19

17

★
10

20

CD-104332

61

Connect the dots from 10 to 25. Start at the ★. Color the picture.

CD-104332 © Carson-Dellosa

Connect the dots from 15 to 25. Start at the ★. Color the picture.

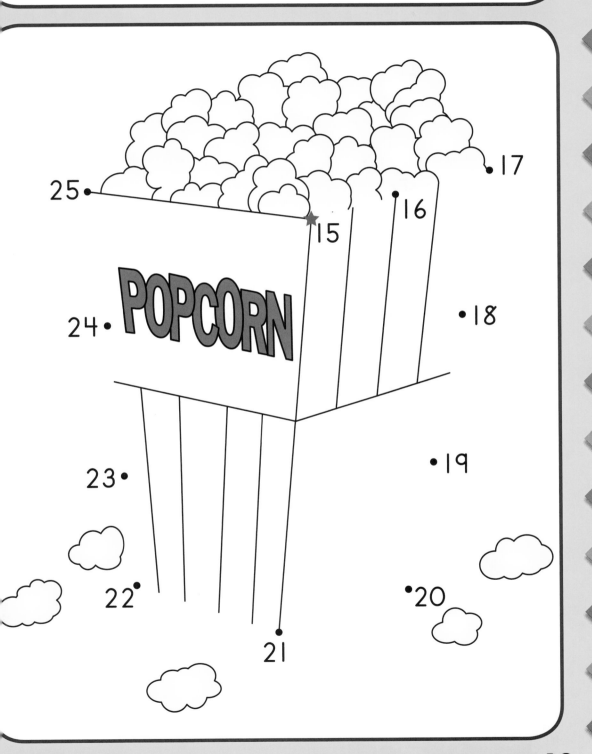

CD-104332 **63**